GREEN JAZZIN' ABOUT

10 jazzy pieces on eco-themes

PIANO/KEYBOARD

PAM WEDGWOOD

FABER *ff* MUSIC

CONTENTS

© 1996 by Faber Music Ltd
First published in 1991 as *Sounds Green* by Faber Music Ltd
3 Queen Square London WC1N 3AU
Music engraved by Sambo Music Engraving Co
Cover by velladesign
Printed in England by Caligraving Ltd
All rights reserved

ISBN 0-571-51645-9

To buy Faber Music publications or to find out about
the full range of titles available please contact your
local music retailer or Faber Music sales enquiries:

Faber Music Limited, Burnt Mill, Elizabeth Way,
Harlow, CM20 2HX England
Tel: +44 (0)1279 82 89 82
Fax: +44 (0)1279 82 89 83
sales@fabermusic.com
www.fabermusic.com

In the 'O' Zone

Save the Whale Waltz

With sadness ♩ = 108

Lead-free Lament

Bottle Bank Boogie

D.S. 𝄋 al ⊕ poi al Coda

(put it in the BANK!)

CODA

poco rit .

trem.

Keep Cool

Litter-bin Blues

Rain Forest Fiesta

Recycled Rag

Green is Beautiful

Rock-on Wildlife

The JAZZIN' ABOUT Series

PAMELA WEDGWOOD

Christmas Jazzin' About. Piano   ISBN 0-571-51507-X

Christmas Jazzin' About. Piano Duet   ISBN 0-571-51584-3

Christmas Jazzin' About. Violin   ISBN 0-571-51694-7

Christmas Jazzin' About. Cello   ISBN 0-571-51695-5

Christmas Jazzin' About. Flute   ISBN 0-571-51586-X

Christmas Jazzin' About. Clarinet   ISBN 0-571-51585-1

Christmas Jazzin' About. Alto Saxophone   ISBN 0-571-51587-8

Christmas Jazzin' About. Trumpet   ISBN 0-571-51696-3

Easy Jazzin' About. Piano   ISBN 0-571-51337-9

Easy Jazzin' About. Piano Duets   ISBN 0-571-51661-0

Green Jazzin' About. Piano   ISBN 0-571-51645-9

Jazzin' About. Piano   ISBN 0-571-51105-8

Jazzin' About. Piano Duets   ISBN 0-571-51662-9

Jazzin' About. Violin   ISBN 0-571-51315-8

Jazzin' About. Cello   ISBN 0-571-51316-6

Jazzin' About. Flute   ISBN 0-571-51275-5

Jazzin' About. Clarinet   ISBN 0-571-51273-9

Jazzin' About. Alto Saxophone   ISBN 0-571-51054-X

Jazzin' About. Trumpet   ISBN 0-571-51039-6

Jazzin' About. Trombone   ISBN 0-571-51053-1

Jazzin' About Styles. Piano   ISBN 0-571-51718-8

Really Easy Jazzin' About. Piano   ISBN 0-571-52089-8

FABER *ff* MUSIC